S0-AIT-770

ISLAND

OF

LIFE

Donated by
NORTHLAND PUBLISHING COMPANY, INC.
A subsidiary of Justin Industries, Inc.

Including the following corporations:
Acme Brick Company • Featherlite Building Products Corporation
Justin Boot Company • Nocona Boot Company
Tony Lama Company, Inc. • Tradewinds Technologies, Inc.

COYOTE IN WINTER, A SEASON OF PLENTY FOR THESE CRAFTY HUNTERS AND SCAVENGERS.

WHEN DEEP SNOWS BLANKET THE GROUND, WHITE-TAILED DEER FLEE FROM DANGER VIA A SHALLOW RIVER BED.

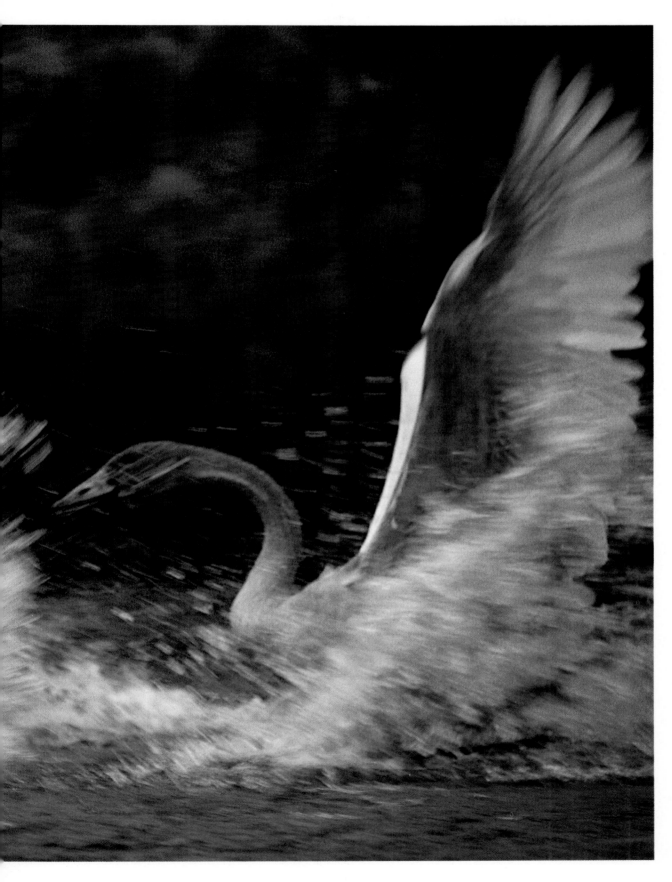

JUVENILE TRUMPETER SWANS PLAY A RUNNING AND FLAPPING GAME, WHICH IMPROVES THEIR TAKE-OFF TECHNIQUE.

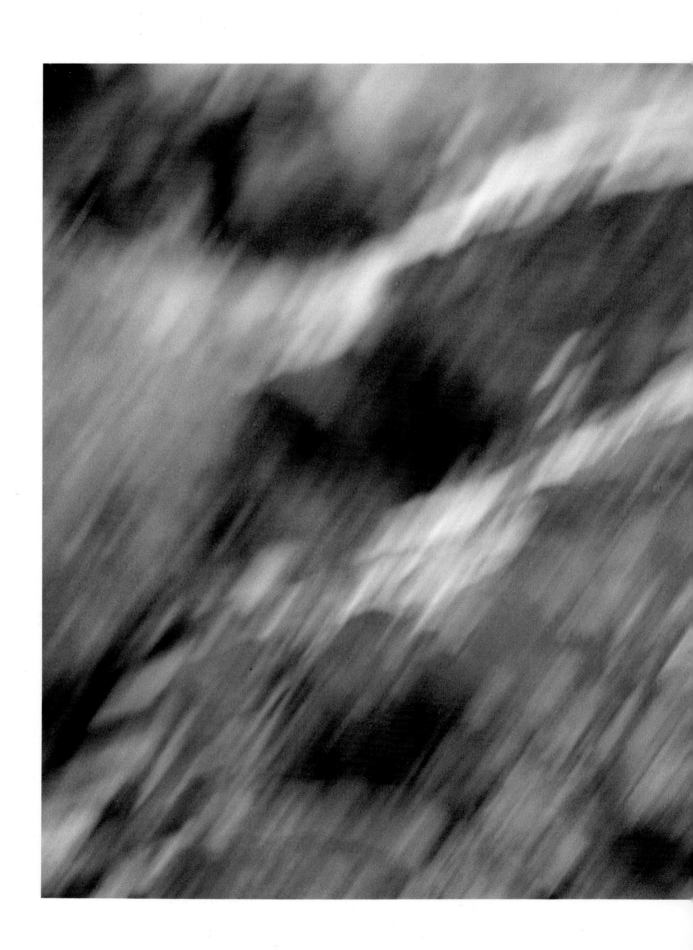

JUST A BLUR IN THE LANDSCAPE, A BOBCAT STREAKS DOWN A ROCKY LEDGE WITH ITS PREY OF RED SQUIRREL.

GRIZZLY BEARS ARE VERY CURIOUS, A BEHAVIORAL TRAIT THAT IS OFTEN INTERPRETED AS AGGRESSION.

ISLAND OF LIFE

WILDLIFE OF GREATER YELLOWSTONE

by

MICHAEL S. QUINTON

Introduction by

GARY TURBAK

NORTHLAND PUBLISHING

FRONTISPIECE: An ancient passing glacier deposited this boulder, which
offers a coyote shelter from the strong winter wind.

Copyright © 1991 by Michael S. Quinton

Introduction copyright © 1991 by Northland Publishing

ALL RIGHTS RESERVED
This book may not be reproduced in whole or in part, by any
means (with the exception of short quotes for the purpose of review),
without permission of the publisher. For information, address
Northland Publishing Co., Post Office Box N, Flagstaff, Arizona 86002.

FIRST EDITION

ISBN 0-87358-524-0

Library of Congress Catalog Card Number 91-52604

Cataloging-in-Publication Data
Quinton, Michael S.
Island of life : wildlife of Greater Yellowstone / by Michael S. Quinton ;
introduction by Gary Turbak. — 1st ed.
144 p.
Includes bibliographical references.
ISBN 0-87358-524-0 : $24.95
1. Mammals—Yellowstone National Park Region—Pictorial works.
2. Birds—Yellowstone National Park Region—Pictorial works. 3. Yellowstone
National Park Region—Pictorial works. I. Turbak, Gary. II. Title.
III. Title: Greater Yellowstone.
QL719.Y45Q55 1991
508.787′52—dc20   91-52604

Designed by Larry Lindahl

Manufactured in Hong Kong by Lammar Press

7.5M/8-91/0352

Contents

ACKNOWLEDGMENTS

*Special thanks to my wife, Cindy;
my sisters, Sharon, Susan, and Tracey; Ty Barker; Leonard Lee Rue III;
Terry McEneaney; Bruce Smith; Bruce Penske; Dick Welch; Brad George;
Blaine Evans; Jeff Brough; Tim Bloxham; Richard Draper; Mike and Kathy
Jenkins; Chuck Trost; Steve Spencer; Robert W. Hernandez;
Ron Shade; and Tim Fitch.*

YELLOWSTONE

A MAGICAL, HUMBLING EXPERIENCE

YELLOWSTONE IS MAGIC. GOOD OLD YOU-WON'T-BELIEVE-your-eyes magic. Rising up out of the plains like a grand mirage, Yellowstone's peaks prod the heavens, and its roots run deep into the bowels of the earth. In great waves of verdant fertility, its forests spread farther than eyes can see. With hissing, steaming, sulfuric glory, it proclaims uncommon power. And like the Garden of Eden, it teems with creatures great and small. Against all odds, the myriad threads of Nature have here woven themselves into a single seamless fabric. This is a place to be remembered and revered. Here, magic is forever in the air. ❖ There is in Yellowstone an overwhelming sense of the primordial, of being present at the creation. Beasts of all breeding walk about, and the earth itself seems unfinished as it belches and smokes with growing pains. The air rushes clear into the lungs, and only the purest of waters course the streambeds. For humans, this is not a place to live, but rather one of Nature's holy sites, where mere mortals come now and then to pay homage. ❖ Half a billion years ago, a giant sea squatted here. Then the Creator's slow-motion hands moved over the waters, and mountains rose from their slumber in the earth. Inside, the mountains seethed, and over the eons great volcanoes three times rearranged the landscape. Six hundred thousand years ago, the last (and

*S*mall geyser along
Twin Lake in Yellowstone National Park. Here,
molten rock left over from ancient eruptions still
seethes and bubbles far underground.

smallest) of these eruptions spewed 240 cubic miles of earth into the sky. A thousand times more powerful than the Mount St. Helens explosion, this blast dumped a foot of ash as far away as Kansas and Nebraska. In Yellowstone, it left entire forests petrified, preserved forever as stone. It also gave Yellowstone its final face-lift (to date, anyway). ❖ The great glaciers of the Wisconsin Ice Age put the finishing touches on Yellowstone, carving and contouring their way across the terrain until even the mountain peaks were covered. When the icy behemoths retreated northward (perhaps as recently as twelve thousand years ago), the stage was finally set for the cornucopia of life that was to follow. ❖ About eleven thousand years ago, the first humans wandered here, perhaps in pursuit of game. Later, their descendants—an Indian tribe called the Sheepeaters—became the first human residents, filling their larders with meat from bighorn sheep. Soon after the turn of the nineteenth century, Lewis and Clark passed by not far from here, but never had more than a hint of the region's wonders. In 1807, an intrepid soul named John Colter became the first Anglo to feast his eyes on Yellowstone. Before long, adventurers such as Jim Bridger also visited here and returned to the East with descriptions of the great splendor and the sometimes-frightening freaks of nature. ❖ Folks greeted the tales of belching mud pots, sulfurous steam, and boiling cauldrons with disbelief—a reaction sometimes encouraged by vivid mountain-man imaginations. Bridger, for example, described the icy-hot contrasts of Yellowstone's waters by claiming to have caught a fish in the cool depths only to have it cooked by boiling water as he pulled it to the surface. Supposedly, he ate it on the spot. ❖ As the years ticked by, however, more people ventured west to see for themselves, and eventually the myth of Yellowstone jelled into reality. With foresight that seems astounding today, Congress and President Ulysses S. Grant in 1872 set aside a portion of the Yellowstone area as a national park—the first in the world. ❖ Today, Yellowstone remains the flagship of America's park system and a model for the rest of the world. Around the globe, hearts beat a little quicker at the sound of that magic-filled word: Yellowstone. The philosophy born here in 1872 has since journeyed to the corners of the earth. Wherever the National Park sign goes up, an unwritten footnote pays homage to Yellowstone, the first of its kind. The revolutionary notion of preserving and protecting huge land tracts and wild menageries may eventually prove to be one of this nation's greatest inventions. ❖ There are, however, really two Yellowstones—an island within an island. At the region's core lies the thirty-five-hundred-square-mile park famous for its geysers and grizzlies and great scenery. This Yellowstone remains sacrosanct, preserved forever as a living monument to the natural world and to human-kind's desire to protect what is wild and free. But the folks who drew the park's boundaries more than a century ago knew little of how natural systems ebb and flow and intertwine. ❖ Consequently, much of the magic of Yellowstone National Park spills out into the surrounding terrain like a horn-of-plenty overflowing. Nearly half of all Yellowstone grizzly habitat lies outside the park. Bison wander like wayward children back and forth across the boundary. Most of the park's elk winter beyond its borders. Rivers, forests, mountain ranges, geothermal features, and the like do not stop at park boundaries. Rather, natural systems seek their own courses throughout a much larger territory, a grand island on the prairie that has come to be called the Greater Yellowstone Ecosystem. ❖ Sprawling over parts of Wyoming, Montana, and Idaho, this com-plex region is six times as large as the park itself and contains as much territory as Vermont, New Hampshire, Delaware, and Rhode Island combined. Greater

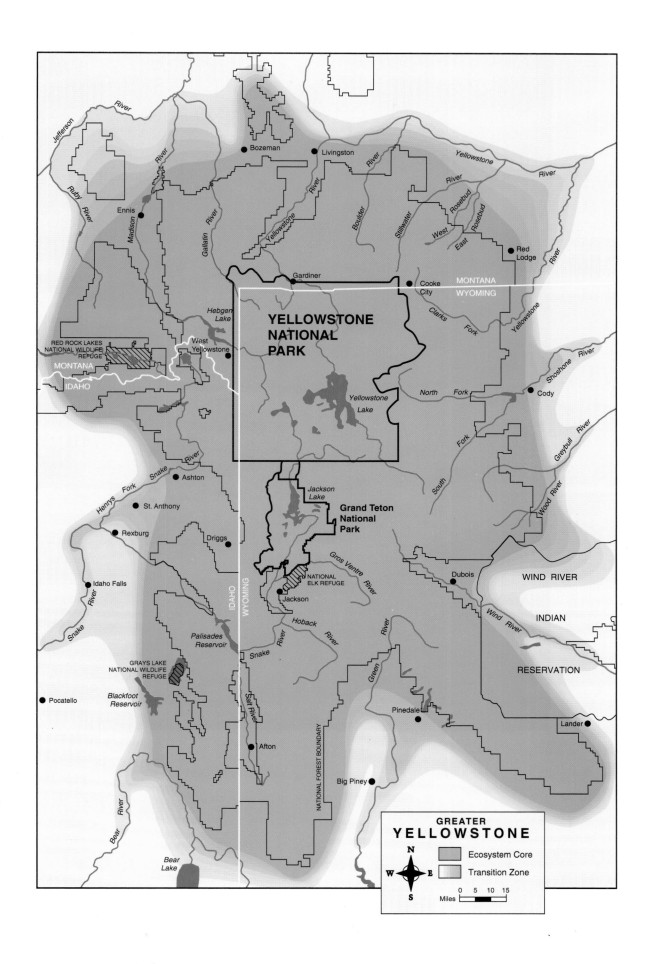

YELLOWSTONE NATIONAL PARK

Grand Teton National Park

RED ROCK LAKES
NATIONAL WILDLIFE
REFUGE

GRAYS LAKE
NATIONAL WILDLIFE
REFUGE

NATIONAL
ELK REFUGE

WIND RIVER

INDIAN

RESERVATION

NATIONAL FOREST BOUNDARY

MONTANA
WYOMING

MONTANA
IDAHO

IDAHO
WYOMING

Jefferson River

Ruby River

Madison River

Gallatin River

Yellowstone River

Boulder River

Stillwater River

West Rosebud

East Rosebud

Rosebud River

Yellowstone River

Clarks Fork

North Fork

South Fork

Shoshone River

Greybull River

Wood River

Wind River

Green River

Gros Ventre River

Hoback River

Snake River

Salt River

Bear River

Snake River

Henrys Fork

Palisades Reservoir

Blackfoot Reservoir

Bear Lake

Hebgen Lake

Yellowstone Lake

Jackson Lake

Bozeman

Livingston

Ennis

Red Lodge

Gardiner

Cooke City

West Yellowstone

Cody

Ashton

St. Anthony

Rexburg

Driggs

Idaho Falls

Dubois

Jackson

Pocatello

Pinedale

Lander

Afton

Big Piney

GREATER
YELLOWSTONE

N
W E
S

▨ Ecosystem Core

▨ Transition Zone

Miles
0 5 10 15

A grizzly makes tracks
across a remote mountainside and through elk calving
grounds. Newborn calves are an important spring food for
grizzly and black bears emerging from hibernation.

Yellowstone is, in fact, the largest eco-system in the northern hemisphere. ❖ But because it is a mishmash of seven national forests, two national parks (Yellowstone and Grand Teton), three wildlife refuges, Bureau of Land Management holdings, and other public and private land in three states, the Greater Yellowstone Ecosystem does not enjoy the protection that Yellowstone Park does. In all, there are thirty different political jurisdictions and an uncounted number of private landowners, many of whom have conflicting ideas about how the region should be managed. Like mice nibbling at the edges of a huge cheese, mining, logging, energy, recreational, and agricultural developments steadily erode the sanctity of the Greater Yellowstone Ecosystem. ❖ As the word "ecosystem" suggests, a natural order governs Yellowstone. There is indeed a system here, a plan, a repeating cycle. Left to itself, Yellowstone embodies a sort of perpetual natural justice—a living, changing, dynamic design that ties each element to every other. Wiser, perhaps, than we humans, Nature concerns itself not with individuals, but with species. When a plant dies to feed the mouse that feeds the coyote, nothing has been lost. When a grizzly's great paws pull a bleating elk calf to the ground, it means the system is working. Coyotes and bears must also eat, and someday their remains will encourage the soil to make more grass to make more mice and more elk. ❖ Topographically, Yellowstone consists of lofty plateaus, gentle valleys, and soaring mountain peaks. It is a high place, with elevations ranging from fifty-two hundred to nearly fourteen thousand feet. (The average elevation is eight thousand feet). Snow is possible during any month, and only July and August are certain to be free of blizzards. Yellowstone Lake and many of the lesser bodies of water freeze up in December and don't lose their icy caps until late May. ❖ Greater Yellowstone is, of course, mountain country, and home to some of the best. The most dominating, perhaps, are the Tetons, which rise with breath-taking majesty along the western edge of Grand Teton National Park. But other ranges—the Absarokas, the Beartooths, the Gallatins, the Madisons, the Centennials—are only slightly less spectacular. Were it possible to subdivide and transport chunks of land, this region could be cut into dozens of parcels, each worthy of being a national park in its own right. ❖ Above ten thousand feet, Yellowstone becomes an open, rocky, windswept place. Trees cannot grow there, and the flowers, grasses and lichens that do exist keep a low profile. Now and then, a hawk or eagle ventures high in search of a pika or marmot lunch, but the alpine country is mostly deserted. ❖ Trickling to life in these highlands are many of the West's most

ebullient rivers—the Madison, Gallatin, Snake, Green, and others. The best of the best is the great Yellowstone River itself, which flows unimpeded 671 miles all the way to its marriage with the Missouri in North Dakota. It is the longest undammed river in the nation—and one of the most beautiful. This cataract quietly exits Yellowstone Lake in the center of the park, makes fertile the sweeping Hayden Valley, then thunders down a pair of magnificent waterfalls

*Cutthroat trout, so named for
the orange slash on their jaws, are the only native trout in the
Greater Yellowstone Ecosystem. Each year, thousands migrate
out of Yellowstone Lake to spawn on a distant sandbar.*

(upper and lower falls are 109 and 308 feet high, respectively) before coursing its way into Montana. ❖ Over the eons, the river has cut into the rhyolite rock a chasm that plunges sixteen hundred feet from rimtop to waterline and ranges from one thousand to four thousand feet wide. The stone walls of the abyss are colored with the yellow of decaying lava, and it is from this hue that early visitors selected the name Yellowstone. ❖ The rivers bring life to the land below. They become the focal point, the gathering place, literally the watering hole for much of Yellowstone's wildlife. Moose stand knee-deep in the shallows, feeding on underwater vegetation. Tiny water ouzels bob along the stream bottoms in search of aquatic insects. Ponderous herds of bison come to quench their prairie thirst. Snipe scurry along the banks. Mallards and great white trumpeter swans laze in the backwaters. ❖ Hundreds of lakes dot this land, led by the jewel-like, 136-square-mile Yellowstone Lake, the largest high-altitude (7,735 feet) water body on the continent. Near its southeast end, a colony of pelicans nest on the tiny Molly Islands, sharing the space with cormorants, terns, and gulls. Ospreys regularly plunge into the clear water, emerging seconds later with a fish gripped tightly in their talons. Eagles swoop low to snatch surface-feeding trout, and other fish-eaters—such as mergansers, herons, and kingfishers—also partake of Yellowstone Lake's abundance. Here and there, a loon sings its haunting, eerie song. Along the 112 miles of shoreline, mink, otters, grizzlies, and black bears seek out the same fishy fare that sustained their ancestors for countless generations. ❖ These waters do indeed teem with fish—native cutthroat trout (so named because of the orange slash on their jaws) and the rainbows, browns, and lake trout that were introduced later. In fact, one of the area's most fascinating wildlife spectacles is the spawning migration out of Yellowstone Lake. Late each spring, thousands of large cutthroats pass in full view of visitors as the fish travel beneath Fishing Bridge (where fishing is not allowed) en route to some secret sandbar where they will lay their eggs. ❖ Although Yellowstone is home to more than a thousand kinds of plants—including glorious wildflowers such as Indian paintbrush, blueflax, monkeyflower, glacier lily, fireweed, and many others—the forests are virtually a monoculture. Some fir and spruce and juniper dot the landscape, but 80 percent of Yellowstone's trees are lodgepole pine, and there are only thirteen tree species in all. With forests covering fully 80 percent of the park, this makes the lodgepole far and away the dominant species. But nutritionally poor soil in some areas puts even the hardy lodgepole to the test— trees two or three centuries old may still measure only a foot in diameter. ❖ Yellowstone is best known, of course, for the surging, belching, steaming erup- tions that issue from its face, sometimes with great power or uncanny regular- ity. The mud pots, fumaroles (a vent that emits only steam), hot springs, and geysers that terrified many early visitors now draw like a magnet travelers from around the globe. Nowhere on earth is there anything like Yellowstone's fantas- tic geothermal fireworks, an unmistakable reminder that volcanoes made—and may one day remake—this region. ❖ Here, molten rock left over from ancient eruptions still seethes and bubbles far underground. From the surface, rain and melting snow seep slowly into this subterranean caldron, traveling through cracks and fissures and porous rock. A mile or more beneath the surface, this water comes under extreme pressure, which allows it to be heated far beyond the boiling point (as high as six hundred degrees) and still remain liquid. When it gets hot enough, the water surges upward with great force until eventually it bursts forth from a geyser or other geothermal exit. Completing the surface-to- depths-to-surface journey may take a century. ❖ Old Faithful, of course, is the most famous of Yellowstone's geothermal gems, sending ten thousand gallons of water 130 feet skyward predictably about once an hour; it has done so longer than anyone has been keeping track—possibly even for centuries. But Yellowstone's internal fury also surfaces in ten thousand other places, and authorities long ago gave up trying to name each geyser and its kin. ❖ It may be geysers that bring people to Yellowstone, but it is the wildlife that causes them to stop their cars and snap their shutters, and fills their memories once they leave. Above all else, Yellowstone means wildlife. Long ago, the clock stopped ticking here, and Yellowstone became stuck in time, locked in an era when plains and forest and mountain teemed with wild creatures. From every corner of the globe people now come to gaze and gasp at this one last giant microcosm of what primitive America once was, a place where all manner of fowl and beast ambled the earth and shared in its bounty. ❖ Yellowstone is indeed a zoo without bars, a menagerie of the first order. Where else can you expect to see—in the course of a single day—free-roaming elk, deer, moose, bison, bighorn sheep, antelope, coyotes, eagles, ospreys, pelicans, swans, geese, and perhaps even a bear or otter? Spend a little more time, look a little closer, and you also may meet additional denizens of the wild world: stately sandhill cranes high-stepping through a meadow, ruffed grouse furiously drumming their wings, a weasel stalking prey only it can see, red squirrels harvesting the forest's bounty, or a great blue heron calmly fishing the shallows. Teal and goldeneyes buzz low over the waters. Gray jays brazenly covet your lunch. Red fox pups roll in mock combat on a meadowed hillside. ❖ If the bestial nations have a commander, if all that is wild and free can be summed up in a single creature, that animal is the grizzly—the potentate of

Yellowstone. It would be difficult to find—anywhere on earth—a species whose presence so dominates its habitat. All other animals give it wide berth, and smart hikers and campers take pains to prevent an encounter with it. The great bear is the first animal people seek when they come to Yellowstone, the one they least want to meet on some lonely trail, and the last one they look for as they leave. The grizzly has become the living symbol of Yellowstone and a metaphor for all

*P*ronghorn fawn lies in the
tall grass. Newborn pronghorns are able to walk within
thirty minutes of birth and can sprint at twenty miles
per hour after two or three days.

wilderness. ❖ Grizzlies are massive creatures full of contradictions. Though the big bruins (a large male may weigh nine hundred pounds) often appear slow and sluggish, they can outrun a horse and can go faster uphill than a human can headed down. A single blow from a grizzly paw can slay an elk, yet the bears spend most of their time grubbing in the dirt for insects and plants to eat. Though easily the most powerful creature on the continent, most grizzlies are shy recluses. ❖ Wandering where it will, the grizzly uses its incredible sense of smell to find food, sometimes following its nose to a rotting carcass two miles away. An old Indian legend says that when a leaf fell in the forest, the eagle saw it fall, the coyote heard it fall, and the grizzly smelled it fall. The great bear spends the warm months eating and putting on the fat that will see it through another frigid winter; and when the days grow short, each bruin seeks out a den and wisely sleeps the cold away. ❖ Once, one hundred thousand grizzlies roamed the western expanses. Fearing no other creature, the great bear went where it would and ate what it found and traveled on. Prairie and river bottom and forest—they were all home to the grizzly. Then came the inexorable march of human feet, the crack of rifles, and the taste of strychnine. Because the bears sometimes ate livestock (or was it because they threatened the human notion of supremacy?), they were hunted down and killed. In a few short decades, grizzlies disappeared from most of the West, with a relative few survivors finding sanctuary in remote and rugged regions. ❖ Today in the United States, healthy grizzly populations exist only in northern Montana along the Continental Divide and in Yellowstone. In all, there are probably fewer than one thousand of the great bears—about two hundred of these in Yellowstone National Park. Here, the bruins are a landlocked clan, isolated by miles of grizzly-less terrain from their nearest cousins. If grizzlies are to survive here—and there is some question about that—they will do it on their own. ❖ Within Yellowstone, the grizzly's story— and that of its smaller cousin, the black bear—has also been marked by human mistakes. Even before the turn of the century, food scraps from hotel restaurants in the park began attracting bears, and authorities soon started using garbage to draw the bruins to viewing stations. In the evenings, tourists assembled to watch a dozen or more grizzlies, eighty-eight was the record, set in 1966) rummage through the trash as rangers talked about the naturalness of Yellowstone. ❖ Things weren't much better elsewhere in the park. Although feeding the bears was forbidden, many visitors did so anyway, and it was not unusual for parents to send their treat-laden children to within a few feet of the bears while the adults snapped photos. The bruins quickly learned to panhandle, and many of them set up more-or-less permanent residence along the park's highways. Bears became Yellowstone's major wildlife attraction, and bear-jams often ground traffic to a halt. In the campgrounds, garbage can lids banged all night long, as both black bears and grizzlies searched for easy meals. ❖ In the late 1960s, authorities came to the realization that it was neither natural nor wise for bears to subsist on handouts and human refuse. They eliminated trash dumps, brought in bear-proof garbage cans, and strictly enforced the prohibition against feeding the animals. Bears that persisted in hanging around humans received a one-way ride deep into the backcountry. In a few years, the bears all but disappeared from sight, as they reverted to a more natural diet of vegetation, carrion, and wild prey. Today, few Yellowstone visitors catch even a glimpse of a bear, although there are about eight hundred in the park (including the two hundred or so grizzlies). ❖ Next to grizzlies, bison are the ecosystem's most awesome creatures. Bulls may weigh a ton, and the cows are not far behind. When dozens of these behemoths erupt from their languid grazing to gallop across the prairie en masse, the sight is one few visitors will ever forget. Yellowstone's bison are direct descendants of the multitudes (perhaps as many as sixty million) that once thundered across the western prairies. Human gluttony and ignorance drove those seemingly inexhaustible herds to the precipice of extinction, and as the nineteenth century wore on, only a few hundred remained in the wild. With amazing luck, many of these animals chose to make their last stand in Yellowstone. ❖ But even here they were not totally safe. In the park's early years, hunting was still permitted, and by the turn of the

Wapiti, or elk, have
adapted to the unforgiving nature of this vast
ecosystem; their trails lead into every forest sanctuary,
over every mountain pass, and across every stream.

century the Yellowstone bison count had dwindled to about fifty head. To prevent the inbreeding that could complete the destruction, authorities bought twenty bison from ranchers who were attempting to domesticate the animals and released them in the park. Today, the Yellowstone bison—numbering about twenty-three hundred—constitute the largest free-roaming, unfenced herd in the nation. ❖ By far the most numerous large animal in Yellowstone is the wapiti, or elk. For more than two millennia, these old-world animals have traveled their ancient migration routes from high-country summer meadows to sheltered winter valleys. No fewer than six separate herds call Yellowstone National Park home, and in a good year the census might include thirty-one thousand animals. ❖ Although elk—especially the bulls with their majestic, spreading antlers—are popular with visitors year-round, they put on their best show in the fall. In early September, autumn's diminishing daylight triggers massive changes in elk hormonal chemistry and the annual rutting ritual begins. The bull's neck swells and his metabolism rises. He becomes cantankerous and restless. With his massive antlers he rips the bark from trees and pitches chunks of sod in the air. Sex replaces food as his greatest need. Rolling in mud and spraying his own belly with urine, he becomes a roving, pungent dynamo of sexual energy. And he bugles. ❖ The voice begins low and reedy deep inside the bull's chest, rises to high-scale clarity, then tumbles downward to its guttural finale. It is an unmistakable, one-of-a-kind sound—a sort of amalgamation of flute, French horn, and bagpipe, trailing off to end in a few grunting snorts from a tuba. ❖ Bugling may release pent-up sexual excitement. More important, it announces—to nearby elk of both sexes—that the bull is ready for breeding. To the cows, this serves as an invitation to join the harem. To other bulls, the bugle is a proclamation of dominance—real or would-be. For every bull with cows, there are several without, and the woods ring with bugling as the haves and the have-nots spar with sound. ❖ The aural pageantry of bugling elk has come to represent the essence of autumn in the high country. If this sound had a smell, it would be of burning leaves. Colored, it might shine like the gold of larch needles in October. If you could feel this bestial music, it would nip at the skin like hoarfrost. No other activity in the wild world so precisely defines a season as does the throaty eloquence of elk in autumn. ❖ When two bulls are evenly matched, vocal battles may give way to physical clashes. Like 750-pound sumo wrestlers, the pair lock antlers, each attempting to push the other backward into defeat. For yards around, their hooves chew the sod into dust. On rare occasions, an antler tip may plunge between an opponent's ribs, inflicting lethal damage. Nature's purpose in all this, of course, is to have the biggest, strongest bulls mate with the cows and pass their genes on to the next generation. ❖ A few weeks after it all began, the bugling and breeding cease, and the bulls, gaunt and tired from the rut, drift off to put on a few pounds before the snow flies. Some elk spend the entire winter in Yellowstone along the Madison and Firehole rivers or in the ambient warmth of a geyser basin. Many, however, migrate out of the highlands to the relative comfort of a valley floor. ❖ The most famous of these wandering herds is the throng of several thousand that converge each winter in the valley lowlands of the National Elk Refuge near Jackson Hole, Wyoming. Here, human development has destroyed their traditional winter range, and authorities have decided to feed the animals. After a winter of relative ease, the wapiti return again to the mountains of southern Yellowstone. ❖ Another animal with a showy mating ritual is the bighorn sheep, about three hundred of which live in Yellowstone. Visitors braving the late fall cold may be treated to a fantastic display as bighorn rams joust for breeding rights to the ewes. After backing off a few dozen yards, competing rams suddenly turn toward each other and charge at speeds up to thirty miles per hour. The sound of two heavy-horned heads smashing together may echo for a mile or more. After a few such clashes, one ram invariably concedes, and the air again becomes still—until the next upstart arrives. Fortunately, nature has given bighorns a highly cushioned skull that prevents serious injury. ❖ Less spectacular are the hundreds of moose that calmly eat their lives away, often while standing knee-deep in a lake or river. Yellowstone also harbors a herd of nearly five hundred pronghorn antelope, America's fastest land animal, and substantially more mule deer. White-tailed deer are rare within the park, but they do inhabit other nearby areas, especially the river bottoms. ❖ Birds, from the calliope hummingbird weighing only a tenth of an ounce to twenty-pound Canada geese, abound in Yellowstone—more than two hundred species in all. Some, like great gray owls and pelicans, often remain far from the paths most people travel. Others—magpies, ravens, and Clark's nutcrackers, to name a few—actually seek out humans in the hope of snatching a free meal. Most simply go about the business of being eagles, tanagers, meadowlarks, or whatever. ❖ Perhaps the most magnificent bird in Yellowstone is the trumpeter swan, the largest waterfowl species in the world. Once, these great birds—which weigh up to twenty-eight pounds and have a wingspan of eight feet or more—flew unmolested across America. No one knows for sure, but they may have numbered in the hundreds of thousands. As pioneers settled the West, however, more and more swans fell before the guns of market hunters, who wanted the birds' glorious plumage for pillows, pens, and adornments. ❖ By 1932, fewer than seventy of the birds remained in the United States, many of them living in the Red Rock Lakes area of Montana, not far from Yellowstone Park's western edge. With protection—including the designation of Red Rock Lakes as a wildlife refuge—the number of swans began to rise, and today about twelve thousand of the magnificent birds grace North America's skies. A few hundred of these remain year-round in Yellowstone and its environs. ❖

Not all animals have always been welcome here. Until rather recently, both wildlife experts and casual observers considered some animals—deer, elk, moose, and the like—to be good and others—wolves, cougars, and coyotes—to be bad. Park managers were no exception, and in one of Yellowstone's saddest chapters, authorities persecuted most large predators and attempted to drive them from the park. Reasoning that fewer predators meant more of everything else, the army (which managed Yellowstone at that time) shot, trapped, and poisoned the meat-eaters with thorough dedication. By 1908, cougars had been virtually exterminated, and sometime in the 1920s, wolves howled for the last time in Yellowstone. Coyotes survived only because of their numbers and their clever nature. ❖ Today, of course, more enlightened thinking prevails, and predators are valued as a vital component of the ecosystem. The ubiquitous coyotes frequently can be seen hunting for mice and voles in Yellowstone's grassy meadows, and on moonlit nights, campers drift to sleep listening to their eerie howls. A few cougars and bobcats now ply their trade here, and occasionally

someone spots a wolverine. The premier predator—the wolf—is still absent, however, and a political battle currently rages over whether wolves should be reintroduced to the ecosystem. ❖ Yellowstone has benefitted greatly from the hands-off, laissez-faire management that allows nature to rule. In the summer of 1988, however, this philosophy underwent the test of fire—literally. During the park's first century, authorities attempted to extinguish every fire in the park,

*A young mountain lion, or
cougar, peers over a rocky ledge. Stalking prey at night,
wild cats take advantage of natural cover before lunging with
lightning speed. The cougar, much larger than the bobcat,
hunts large prey such as deer and elk.*

even employing a bear named Smokey to personify the "put-it-out" policy. This worked well enough, but gradually ecologists came to realize that fire is as natural a part of Yellowstone as bears and bison. For eons, fire has come to Yellowstone like the seasons, each time clearing away the old and making a place for the new. Preventing dead wood from burning one year only preserves more fuel for the next fire season. In the 1970s, there went into effect a "let-burn" policy that allowed most blazes to run their natural course. ❖ The fall of 1987 was very dry, and when expected rains did not arrive the next July, all it took was a few lightning strikes to ignite a tinder-dry Yellowstone. Over the next three months, wind-whipped fires spread across more than three-quarters of a million acres of the park, burning countless trees but killing surprisingly few animals: only three hundred forty-five elk, thirty-six deer, twelve moose, nine bison, and six black bears are known to have perished in the blazes. The scenery took the biggest beating, and blackened stands of timber remain today as testimony to the fire's rage. ❖ Though it may seem destructive to human eyes, fire is really a beginning, not an end. Just a few months after blazes blackened huge chunks of Yellowstone, carpets of green—seedlings, flowers, grasses—peeked through the embers. Fed by the nutrients released in the blaze and now open to the sun, this new growth fattens elk and deer, which will in turn put meat on coyote and grizzly bones. In Yellowstone, nothing is wasted. ❖ Even the forest that seems so devastated has, with fire, bought a new lease on life. Lodgepole pine, the dominant tree in the park, has lived with fire so long that it has evolved two kinds of cones. One type opens normally at the end of the growing season to spread its seeds to the wind. The other, however, remains tightly closed—for many years if necessary—until heated to 140 degrees or so. Like little time capsules, these cones lie on the forest floor until fire sweeps through and liberates their pent-up reproductive potential. Following the 1988 conflagration, up to twenty lodgepole seeds per square foot showed up in some areas, and soon there may be one thousand trees per acre to replace those lost in the blaze. ❖ Without a doubt, the wonders of Yellowstone provide incomparable treats for our senses. This great land also performs an additional service that may be the most important of all: It inspires humility. ❖ Virtually everything about Yellowstone is large and grand. The mountains are tall, the waterfalls high, the lakes immense, and the terrain vast. Even the wildlife—many species, at least—are big. So is the sky. The rivers are swift and strong, and the power of the geysers, awesome. Truly, this is a land apart, a wild world without equal. ❖ Amid this greatness, humans stand meek and muted. Here, each of us is but a speck, a tiny trespasser on a great natural tapestry. Standing on a windswept Yellowstone ridge or at the edge of a perpetually rushing river, our true importance shifts into focus. Our puffed-up self-worth shrinks into perspective. Above all else, Yellowstone is a humbling experience—and that is good.

PEAKS &
PLATEAUS

THE MOUNTAINS OF THE GREATER YELLOWSTONE
Ecosystem—including the Tetons, Beartooth, Gallatins, Madisons,
and Absarokas—are rugged and isolated, but offer wilderness sanctuary for those species able to meet the challenges. Few animals can
successfully survive the steep, jagged cliffs, high, forceful winds, and year-round
snow typical of this alpine habitat. ❖ Bighorn sheep and mountain goats are
the animals most commonly associated with the alpine habitat, yet only
the goats are year-round residents. Bighorn sheep summer in the alpine
environment but generally retreat to lower elevations for the winter (there
are exceptions). The smaller pika and yellow-bellied marmots make their
homes in boulder-strewn mountain basins, gathering dry grasses and wildflowers to line their dens. The largest of Yellowstone's squirrels, marmots
may spend eight months each year in hibernation, while pikas stay active all
year. They are quick to alert other wildlife of approaching danger with
whistles and blasts. ❖ Many species—elk, grizzly bears, mule deer, bobcats,
mountain lions, and more—range across the mountain peaks and plateaus,
but few call this alpine environment home. ❖ *OPPOSITE: Bighorn sheep, ram
and ewe. ABOVE: Pika, also called a rock rabbit, whistles near its rock-pile nest.*

*Elk calf springs along
a mountainside. As the snow melts, cows lead
their calves back into the high mountain pastures where
they will stay until the first snow of autum.*

*Windswept and snow-
covered mountain peaks, like the Beartooth Mountains
(above), are home to a handful of introduced mountain goats
(left). These mammals are the only year-round residents
living above timberline, and sightings are rare.*

*Bighorn sheep vie for dominance
in the upcoming rut. Arguments are settled with terrific head-on
collisions that leave the rams dazed. Splintered horns and
bloody noses are common, but fatalaties are rare.*

*Bighorn ewes and lamb (above).
Ewes retreat to the tundra during spring and summer to rear their
lambs and feed on new plants. Lambs are born in April, usually
one per ewe, and are able to climb steep cliffs within a day or
two. A black-billed magpie (opposite) perches on a young
bighorn sheep. Magpies are adapted to grassland habitats but
require trees for nesting.*

*T*he Clark's nutcracker (opposite)
lives near mountaintops year-round, but is sometimes forced to
the forests or developed areas during severe winters. Its preferred
food is whitebark pine nuts. A yellow-bellied marmot(above)
gathers grasses to line its rocky mountain den.

*Mule deer buck gently nuzzles
a doe. The buck displays his antlers to the doe in heat from
every angle to entice her to mate. A buck's antlers tell more about
his general health and vigor than his age. A buck will grow
his largest antlers in the prime of life.*

FOREST
SANCTUARY

BECAUSE OF THE GREAT DIVERSITY OF WILDLIFE FOUND in the Greater Yellowstone Ecosystem, one might expect an equally diverse forest community. Yet, just the opposite is the case: The forest community is essentially a monoculture dominated by the lodgepole pine. Found from elevations of seven to ten thousand feet, this slow-growing tree needs fire to reproduce. The cones remain tightly closed—for years if necessary—until the heat of a forest fire causes them to open. The seeds then fall to the ground, and a new forest grows. Competing species do not invade an established lodgepole pine forest because they cannot tolerate the nutritionally poor, well-drained soils or the low precipitation (twenty to forty inches annually). ❖ Lodgepole pine forests provide critical habitat for great gray owls, who build nests in the snags of dead, standing trees—in fact, the owls' existence depends on finding suitable nesting sites in these snags, for no other tree will do. Grizzly bears, snowshoe hares, pocket gophers, long-tailed weasels, jumping mice, and a variety of birds are all important residents of the forest sanctuary. ❖ *OPPOSITE: A bull elk reaches to nibble the boughs of a well-browsed Douglas fir. ABOVE: The gray jay is a year-round resident of greater Yellowstone.*

*F*orcing air out of bright red air
sacks, the male blue grouse makes a low-sounding call to his
mate. Once he has lured the female to him, he struts his
plumage as part of a courtship display.

*The male ruffed grouse attracts
females by drumming his wings, creating a thumping sound
irresistible to female ruffed grouse. The males are especially active
at dawn and dusk, but may be heard at any hour.*

The pine grosbeak is a nomadic
traveler in search of seeds and pinecones. During snowy winters,
these birds scatter throughout the forest, but remain in contact with
the flock by calling their characteristic three-noted whistle.

A Williamson's sapsucker
with a billful of ants is bound for its nest of hungry chicks.
This particular bird, like other forest dwellers, had its nest
in an excavated cavity of a large aspen tree.

*The Steller's jay is a year-
round resident who caches pine nuts and seeds for the long
winter. This jay inhabits only the western regions of North
America, from Alaska into Central America.*

*Ravens have a close relationship
with the predators of greater Yellowstone and will flock around
an animal within hours of its death. If carrion is not available,
they will often look for dead fish along lakeshores and
streamsides, or search for seeds and insects.*

A warbling verio
sings a few yards from its nest in an aspen sapling.
This is one of many bird species who are
summer residents only.

*An adult female robin
brings food—grasshopper, spider, caterpiller—for her
chicks, though only the most aggressive—the widest
mouth—will be rewarded.*

*A female great gray owl
and her three-week-old chick sit atop their nest, an old
dished-out lodgpole pine snag. Female great gray owls
are larger and more aggressive than the males.*

Great horned owlets at
five weeks old are ready to fledge. This winged predator
feeds on grouse, hares, mice, ducks, other owls, and skunks
and is a year-round resident of the forest.

*Pocket gophers are the great
gray owl's main prey. Perched high in a tree, a great gray
uses its ears and a method of triangulating sound to locate
the tiny underground prey. Then, with lightning speed,
the owl plunges to the ground for the kill,
which is consumed whole.*

*The golden-mantled ground
squirrel (opposite) lives in rock slides and cliffs throughout
the ecosystem. This ground squirrel looks like a chipmunk
(above), but is larger, measuring approximately ten inches,
and does not have stripes on its face. The squirrel eats
primarily seeds, leaves, buds, and roots.*

*The long-tailed weasel (above)
is a carnivore whose favorite foods include mice, voles, bird eggs,
and insects. A red squirrel (opposite) pries off the tough scales of
a lodgepole pinecone to get the tiny seeds inside. Red squirrels
cache nuts and seeds, especially those of whitebark pine trees.*

*M*artens travel wide circuits
through the forest in search of their favorite prey–squirrels.
They also hunt voles, snowshoe hares, grouse,
porcupines, and chipmunks.

*P*orcupines are covered with
sharp, barbed quills that protect them from attack. They
graze on grasses, shrubs, clover, and wildflowers in the
summer and eat tree bark during the winter.

*A large black bear takes
possession of a winter-killed elk. Black bears often feed on
carrion upon emerging from hibernation because they don't have
to expend much energy to secure it. This bear lays on the carcass
to keep hungry ravens from sharing his meal.*

*The vast forests of the Greater
Yellowstone Ecosystem have saved grizzly bears from extirpation
and provide a sanctuary where they can live relatively undisturbed.
Grizzlies have adapted to the many life zones of this ecosystem
and range from the dry lowlands to the high alpine tundra.
The forest provides much of the bears' diet, including grasses,
ants, bugs and grubs, berries, pine nuts, pocket gophers, and
carrion. Grizzlies obtain most of their food by digging—their
powerful shoulders, arms, and long talons make easy
work of earth moving. This omnivore has only one
natural enemy—HOMO SAPIENS.*

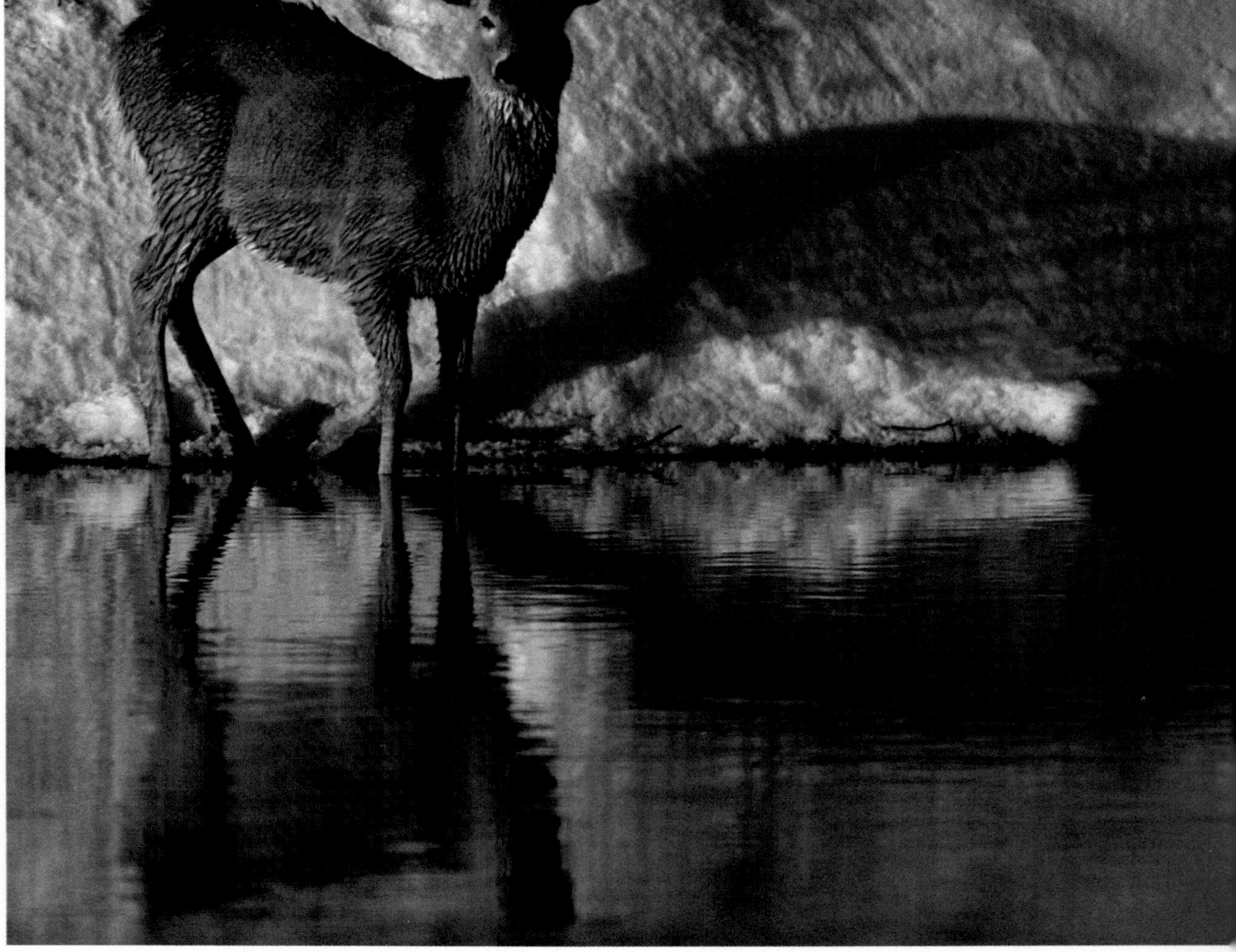

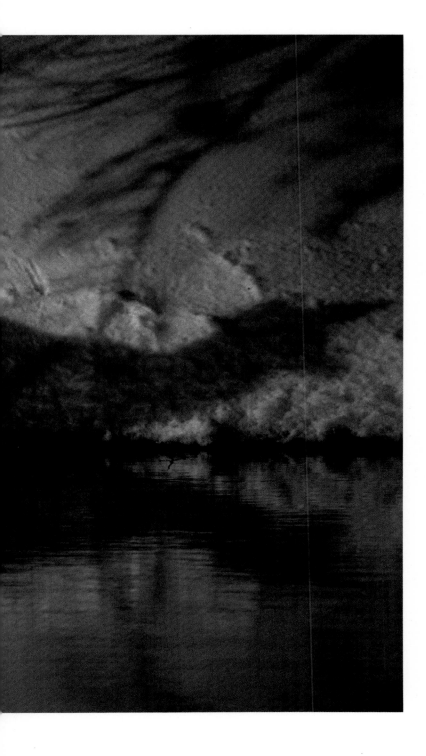

A white-tailed deer
casts a long winter shadow across the snowbank.
The river, shallow and ice-free, offers a safe niche in a
harsh wintery world. White-tails feed on aquatic
plants and even bed down in shallow water.

*By far the most regal of North
America's great wild creatures, the Rocky Mountain bull elk
may carry twenty pounds of antlers for up to 140 days before
declining hormone levels cause them to loosen and fall off.*

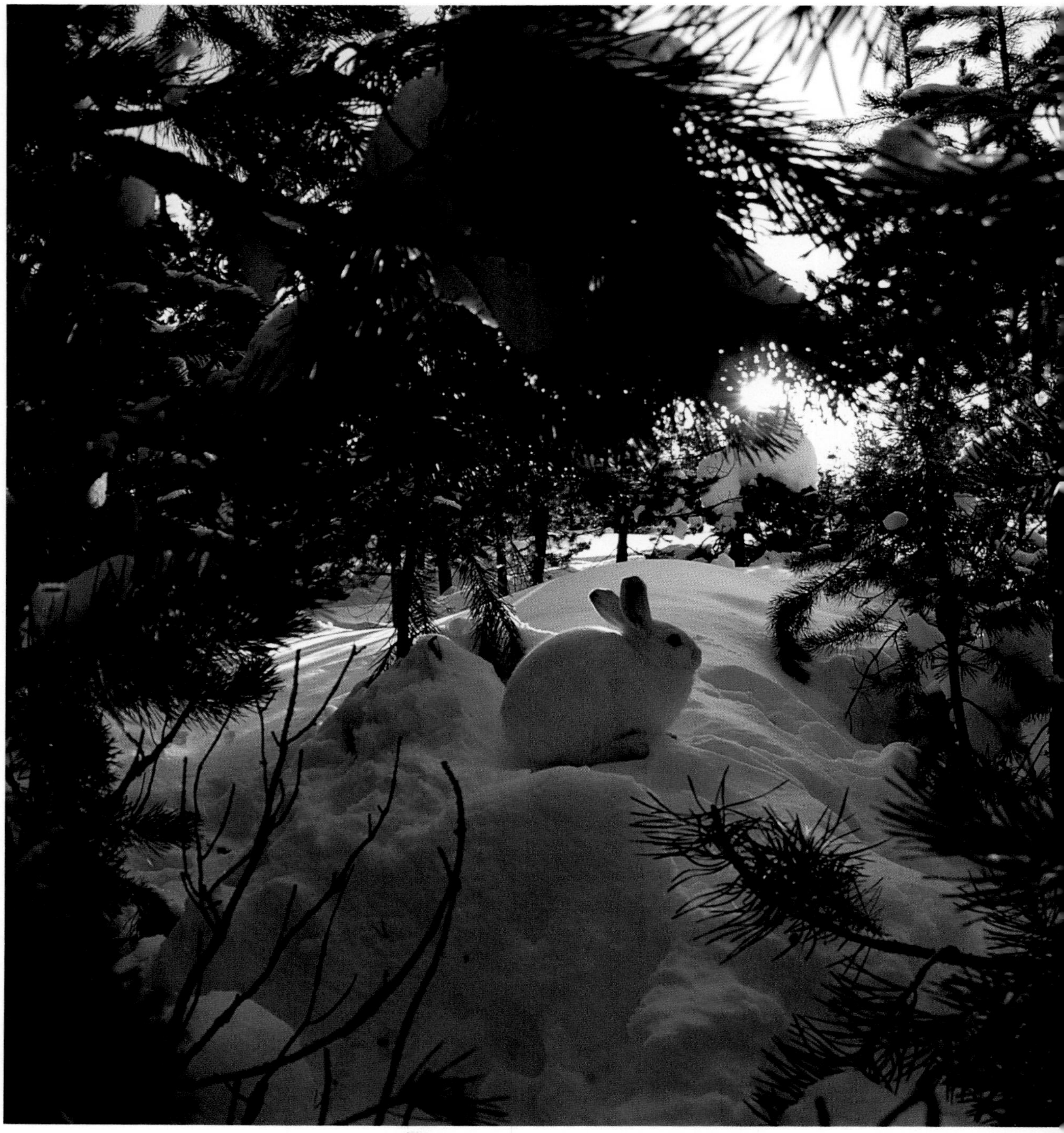

*Named for its large hind
feet, the snowshoe hare survives a long list of predators
by blending into the scenery.*

*Where snow persists into late
May and June, a hare may find itself completely molted
into summer brown and without the protection
of its natural camouflage.*

A snowshoe hare
pauses during its late-summer evening
search for clover and other browse.

Mountain
Meadows

W HETHER ALPINE MEADOW OR SAGEBRUSH GRASSLAND, the open spaces of the Greater Yellowstone Ecosystem support the tiniest birds and mice as well as the mammoth bison. Native grasses and wildflowers flourish during the warmest months of the year; they provide food, nesting material, and hiding places for seasonal and year-round wildlife residents. ❖ Birdlife of the mountain meadows includes the American goldfinch, a seasonal resident. Studies of winter migration indicate that this avian creature is reluctant to fly over water; in one case, an entire flock returned to shore after realizing they were over water. Only an extreme drop in temperature finally convinced the chattering birds to again take wing. ❖ Where even the lowest elevations are above six thousand feet, the growing season is short and summer's beauty, passing. Although mountain meadows support life, they can also become the killing grounds for a winter-weakened animal surrounded by coyotes. Such are the checks and balances of the natural world. ❖ *OPPOSITE: Dressed in its subtle fall colors, a goldfinch feeds on dried wildflower seeds. ABOVE: Mule deer doe. Mule deer may be found almost anywhere in the ecosystem.*

*Red fox pups gather
to watch from the opening of their underground
den for the adults returning with ground
squirrels, voles, or small birds.*

*D*oe mule deer and twins emerge from
the forest for evening browsing. Does and fawns may be seen foraging in
open forests and meadows, searching for their favorite foods, serviceberry and
honeysuckle leaves, although here they are nibbling elk thistle and sage.

*Young pronghorn buck. An
adult pronghorn is considered the fastest land mammal,
able to achieve a speed of fifty miles per hour.*

*Bull elk patrols his harem
in a smoky meadow along the Madison River. Autumn
marks the height of rutting season, when bulls care
only about keeping a harem and mating.*

MOUNTAIN

MEADOWS

79

Evening primrose adds
to the color and variety of meadow wildlife. The elk calf,
unable to outrun its enemies for the first few days of life, lies low
and still and is easily overlooked by predators. The cow elk
is aggressive in driving away any potential enemy
that comes too close to her calf.

*A cow bison leads her new
calf on its first steps along a journey through an uncertain life.
Bison are the largest land mammals on the continent
and were once the most numerous.*

*Bison bull winters in the
deep snow of a high mountain valley. As winter loses
its grip, chances for survival increase daily.*

A long-tailed weasel
dons its winter coat. Like snowshoe hares, weasels
are brown during the summer and change to white during
winter. This seasonal change provides camouflage both
when hunting prey and avoiding predation.

A coyote's tracks are etched
into a wind-blown drift as this wily hunter mouses along
a frozen river, ears cocked, listening for the subtle
sounds of voles under the snow.

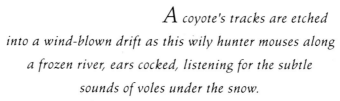

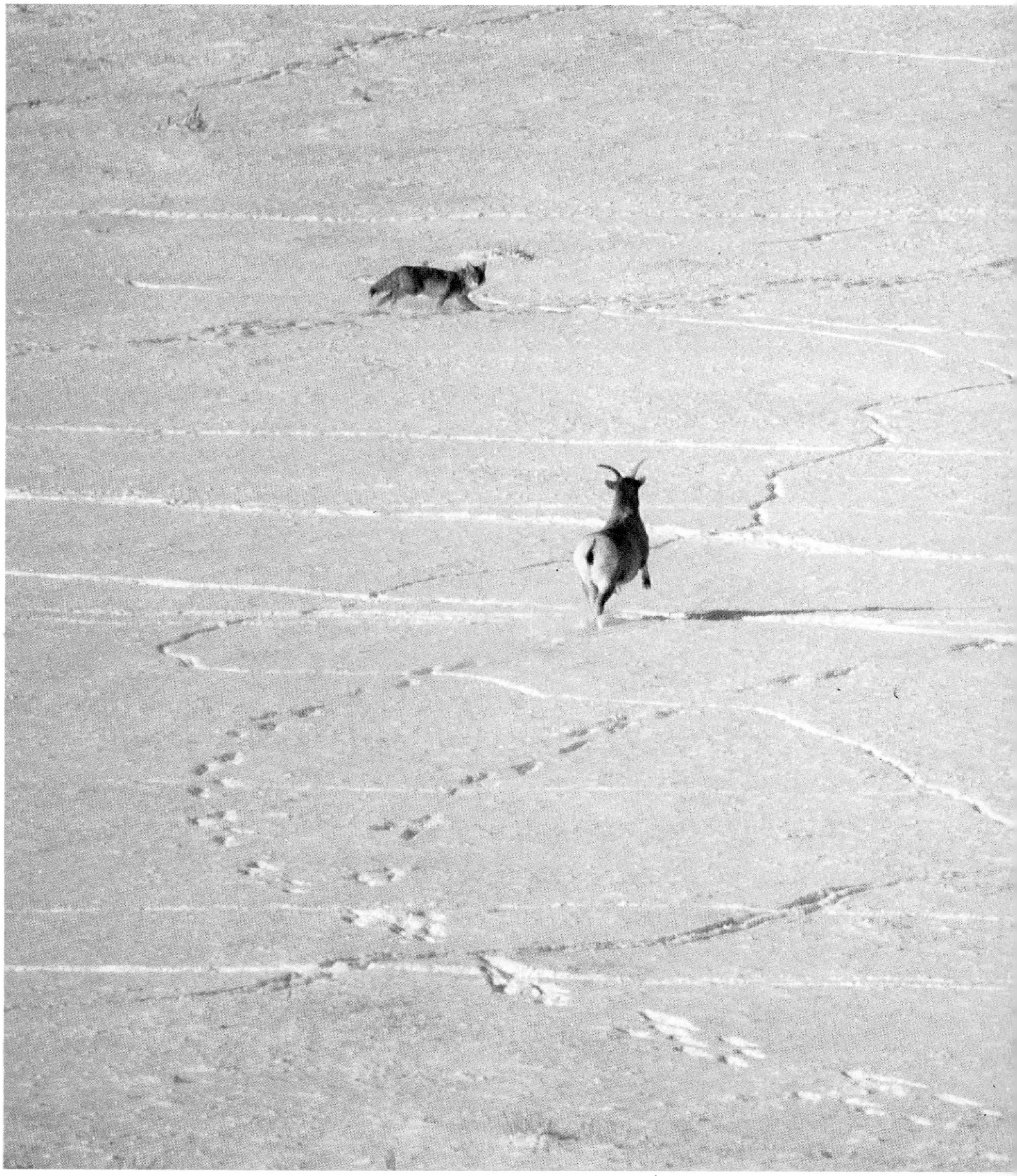

*Packs of coyotes often cooperate
to bring down large prey like bighorn sheep: one coyote chases
the sheep in the direction of his waiting accomplices.*

*C*oyotes chew and tug on their
prey, a calf elk killed by the pack. Tracks in the snow told a
horror story of death: the coyotes had harassed the calf through
the night, while the cow kept the pack from finishing the job until
morning. In all, about a dozen coyotes shared in the kill. The
death of the calf brought life not only to the coyotes but also to a
gathering of ravens, magpies, and gray jays. With seamless
perfection, nature provides balance in a life and death
struggle where the weak and unfit do not survive.

Winter's long silence is
shattered with the return of the sandhill cranes. These
birds fly in family flocks of twenty to one hundred,
forming a characteristic V shape as they travel.

*The cranes arrive on their
breeding grounds in pairs and establish a nesting territory
in wild marshes and meadows. They bow and dance before
mating and build a nest on the ground using whatever materials
are available—usually cattails, willows, grasses, or sticks.
Both adults incubate the brown, speckled eggs and care
for the chicks. Adult cranes will feign injury
to lure danger away from the nest.*

LAKES &
TRIBUTARIES

THE RIVERS—YELLOWSTONE, MADISON, GALLATIN, AND
Snake—and lakes—Shoshone, Lewis, Yellowstone, and Jackson—of the
Greater Yellowstone Ecosystem provide pristine habitat to seasonal
(white pelican, snowy egret), migratory (tundra swan, red-necked grebe), and
year-round (beaver, American dipper) wildlife residents. While these watery
habitats are obviously critical to the region's only native trout—the
cutthroat—who spawn in the turbulent river waters, and the majestic trumpeter swans, who nest on islands in the shallow, mirrorlike lakes, they are
equally important to the moose, bald eagle, and grizzly bear. The life-sus-
taining qualities of these waterways extend not only to water-dwelling creatures,
but also to every member of the plant and animal communities. ❖ As winter
byways for white-tailed deer, icy playgrounds for river otters, nesting territories
for common loons, or spawning grounds for cutthroat trout, the lakes and
tributaries of greater Yellowstone mean survival. ❖ *OPPOSITE: Cutthroat trout
swim upstream each spring to spawn. ABOVE: A female red-necked grebe, a summer
resident only, incubates eggs on the nest.*

*A*crobatic spotted sandpipers
walk lightly across lily pads while foraging for small insects,
snails, and assorted larvae. In a courting mood, sandpipers
form a pair-bond prior to building a small grass nest
on dry ground amidst concealing vegetation.

*Harlequin ducks return from the sea
each spring to the fast-running rivers of Yellowstone. These ducks are the rarest
breeding waterfowl in the ecosystem. They feed by diving in the strong current and
plucking insects, larvae, snails, and aquatic plants from the stream bottom.*

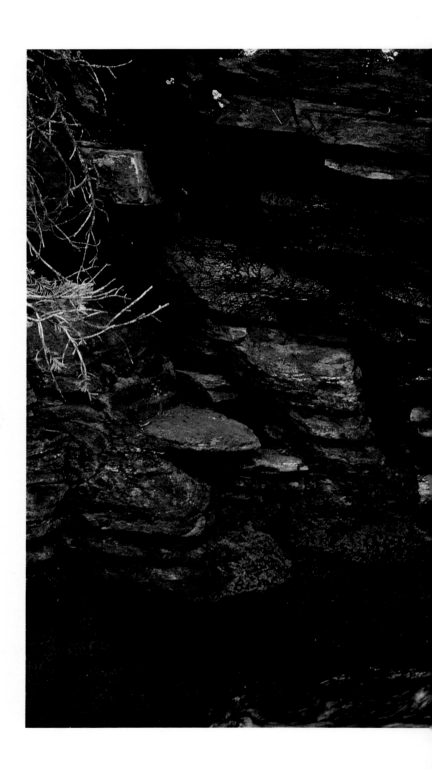

*T*hree bright yellow, gaping mouths reach
out through the hole in their moss nest as an adult dipper appears with a
billful of insects. Dippers dive into fast-flowing creeks and rivers for
insects and larvae, small minnows, and crustaceans.

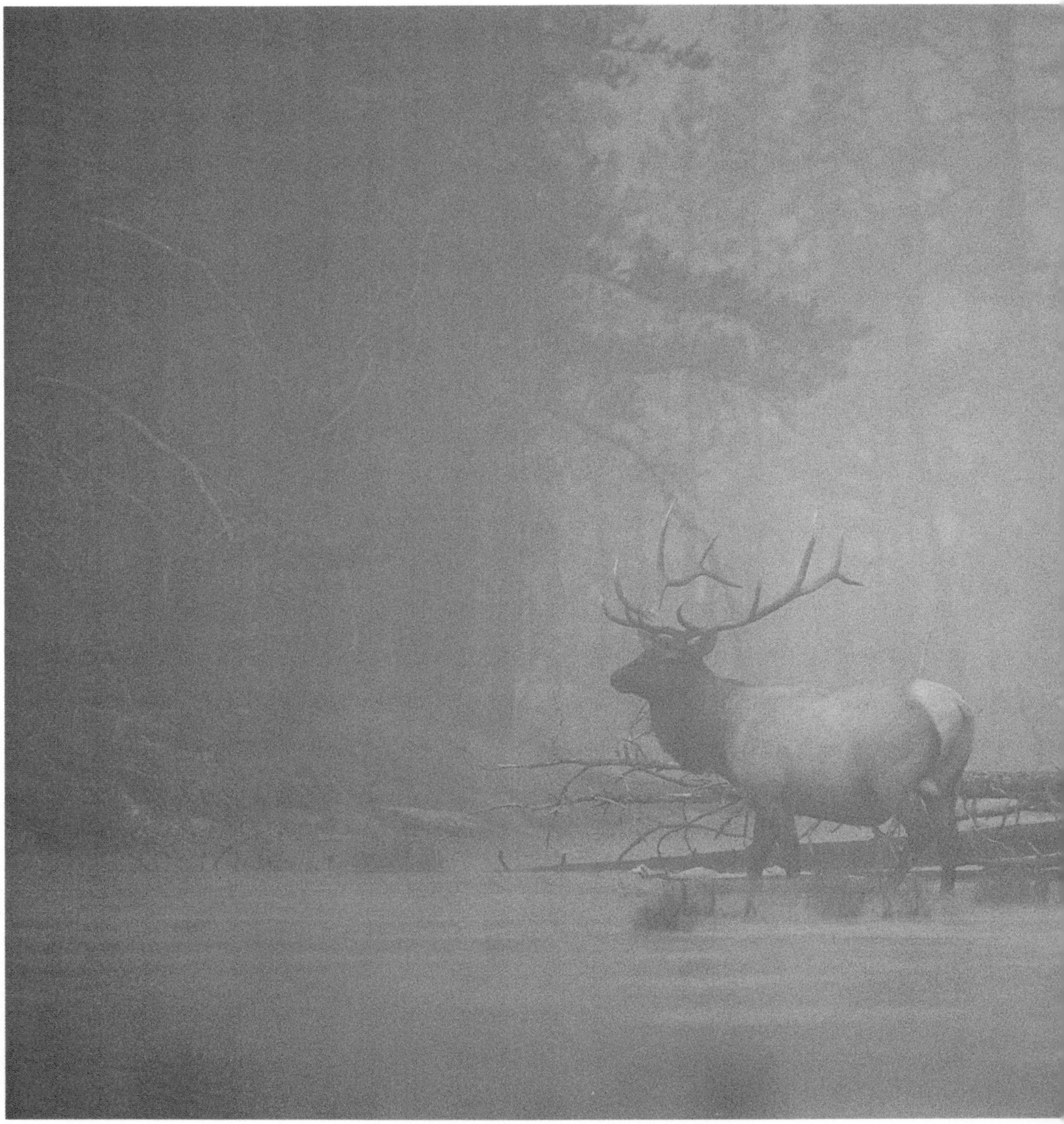

*The fires in Yellowstone
National Park during the summer of 1988 and the
subsequent long, hard winter were a deadly combination
for many elk. Ultimately, the weak and ill were eliminated,
clearing the way for the strong and healthy.*

A white-tailed deer canters
along a shallow river bed. These deer are not as common in

*the ecosystem as the larger mule deer, and are nonmigratory,
wintering in relatively small areas of prime habitat.*

*By early autumn, the
Shiras bull moose have grown new antlers and begin
to shed the velvet. As the rut begins, bulls become quite
aggressive and engage in powerful shoving matches.*

A day-old common loon chick
peaks out from under its mother's tail feathers. The Greater
Yellowstone Ecosystem represents the southern limit of breeding
habitat for both the common loon and red-necked grebe.

*Bufflehead ducklings follow
their mother in a small pond. These buffleheads had
their nest in the cavity of a nearby tree.*

The characteristic "honking"
call and white cheek patches easily identify Canada geese.
Shallow rivers offer food and nesting areas for these large birds,
who build their nests on islands, in tree stumps, and on cliffs. A
newly hatched chick (opposite) anxiously looks
for its parents, who mate for life.

A *peregrine falcon bathes in icy*
mountain waters. This seasonal resident of greater Yellowstone
challenges ducks with its fast flight and dramatic swoops. Pesticide
accumulation has brought this predator to the brink of extinction: it is
now absent from the eastern United States and scarce in the West.

*Cygnet (juvenile) trumpeter swans
feed on freshwater aquatic plants by plucking them from the bottom
of shallow rivers and lakes. Their long necks, equal to their bodies in
length, enable them to reach food that ducks and geese cannot.
They do not dive underwater like loons.*

*Cinnamon teal preen in the
cool mist of dawn. After hatching, cinnamon teal, like all
ducklings, imprint on their mother's call, which helps keep the
group together on a lake that may support other cinnamon
teal families as well as other waterfowl.*

A great blue heron preens.
These fish-eaters are commonly seen standing in shallow
water or along shorelines. They often make twenty- to
thirty-mile round trips to feed.

*The trumpeter swan is
North America's largest waterfowl: an adult male
may weigh as much as thirty pounds and have a wingspan
of eight feet or more. The Greater Yellowstone Ecosystem is
the only area in the lower forty-eight states where
trumpeters live year-round.*

*A river otter feeds on a long-
nosed sucker. These playful creatures are year-round residents
of greater Yellowstone's lakes and streams, and can maneuver
quite well around and beneath ice flows in winter. Their underground dens, built in the banks of lakes and streams, have
two entrances: one from underwater and one from land.*

*Spawning cutthroat trout
face a number of predators, including coyotes and bald eagles.
The immature eagle (opposite) must feed quickly because it will
soon be harassed by ravens, magpies, and other eagles. Coyotes,
too, will try to steal trout, but are able to catch their own.*

*An adult bald eagle flies
from its perch in a cottonwood tree overlooking a stream
of cutthroat trout. Bald eagles eat carrion and sometimes
crippled waterfowl, but their mainstay is fish.*

REFERENCES

THE AUDUBON SOCIETY FIELD GUIDE TO NORTH AMERICAN BIRDS: WESTERN REGION. New York: Alfred A. Knopf, 1977.

Despain, Don, Douglas Houseon, Mary Meagher, and Paul Schullery. WILDLIFE IN TRANSITION: MAN AND NATURE ON YELLOWSTONE'S NORTHERN RANGE. Boulder, Colorado: Roberts Rinehart, Inc., 1986.

Hansen, Skylar. THE TRUMPETER SWAN: A WHITE PERFECTION. Flagstaff, Arizona: Northland Publishing, 1984.

Larrison, Earl J., and Donald R. Johnson. MAMMALS OF IDAHO. Moscow, Idaho: University Press of Idaho, 1981.

McEneaney, Terry. BIRDS OF YELLOWSTONE. Boulder, Colorado: Roberts Rinehart, Inc., 1988.

Murie, Olaus J. THE ELK OF NORTH AMERICA. Jackson, Wyoming: Teton Bookshop, 1979.

Petersen, David. AMONG THE ELK: WILDERNESS IMAGES. Flagstaff, Arizona: Northland Publishing, 1988.

Scott, M. Douglas, and Suvi A. WILDLIFE OF YELLOWSTONE AND GRAND TETON NATIONAL PARKS. rev. ed. Salt Lake City, Utah: Wheelwright Press, Ltd., 1988.

Streubel, Donald. SMALL MAMMALS OF THE YELLOWSTONE ECOSYSTEM. Boulder, Colorado: Roberts Rinehart, Inc., 1989.

Varley, John D., and Paul Schullery. FRESHWATER WILDERNESS: YELLOWSTONE FISHES AND THEIR WORLD. Yellowstone National Park, Wyoming: The Yellowstone Library and Museum Association, 1983.